The NFL's Greatest Teams

ARIZONA CARDINALS

Big Buddy Books

An Imprint of Abdo Publishing
abdopublishing.com

Katie Lajiness

abdopublishing.com

Published by Abdo Publishing, a division of ABDO, PO Box 398166, Minneapolis, Minnesota 55439.
Copyright © 2017 by Abdo Consulting Group, Inc. International copyrights reserved in all countries. No part
of this book may be reproduced in any form without written permission from the publisher. Big Buddy Books™
is a trademark and logo of Abdo Publishing.

Printed in the United States of America, North Mankato, Minnesota.
092016
012017

Cover Photo: ASSOCIATED PRESS.
Interior Photos: ASSOCIATED PRESS (pp. 5, 7, 9, 11, 13, 14, 15, 17, 18, 19, 20, 21, 23, 25, 28, 29);
    ZUMA Press, Inc./Alamy Stock Photo (p.27).

Coordinating Series Editor: Tamara L. Britton
Graphic Design: Michelle Labatt, Taylor Higgins, Jenny Christensen

Publisher's Cataloging-in-Publication Data

Names: Lajiness, Katie, author.   7019748
Title: Arizona Cardinals / by Katie Lajiness.
Description: Minneapolis, MN : Abdo Publishing, 2017. | Series: NFL's greatest
    teams | Includes bibliographical references and index.
Identifiers: LCCN 2016944875 | ISBN 9781680785265 (lib. bdg.) |
    ISBN 9781680798869 (ebook)
Subjects: LCSH: Arizona Cardinals (Football team)--History--Juvenile literature.
Classification: DDC 796.332--dc23
LC record available at http://lccn.loc.gov/2016944875

Contents

A Winning Team

The Arizona Cardinals are a football team from Phoenix, Arizona. They have played in the National Football League (NFL) for more than 90 years.

The Cardinals have had good seasons and bad. But time and again, they've proven themselves. Let's see what makes the Cardinals one of the NFL's greatest teams.

Red and white are the team's colors.

League Play

Team Standings

The NFC and the American Football Conference (AFC) make up the NFL. Each conference has a north, south, east, and west division.

The NFL got its start in 1920. Its teams have changed over the years. Today, there are 32 teams. They make up two conferences and eight divisions.

The Cardinals play in the West Division of the National Football Conference (NFC). This division also includes the Los Angeles Rams, the San Francisco 49ers, and the Seattle Seahawks.

6

The Seattle Seahawks are a major rival of the Cardinals.

7

Kicking Off

The team was founded in 1898 by businessman Chris O'Brien. It's the NFL's oldest team. The Cardinals won their first NFL **championship** in 1925.

But, the team struggled during the 1930s and 1940s. After **World War II**, the Cardinals rebounded. They won the NFL championship in 1947. The team won the Western Division title in 1948.

CHICAGO CARDINALS
NATIONAL FOOTBALL LEAGUE
1947 — WORLD CHAMPIONS — 1947

Top Row—Caleb Martin, t; Paul Christman, b; Jake Colhouer, g; Pat Harder, b; Bill Campbell, c; Jack Doolan, e; Joe Parker, e; Hamilton Nichols, g; Frank Kriznecky, trainer.
2nd Row—Arch Wolfe, bus. mgr.; Ray "Buddy" Parker, ass't coach; Bill Blackburn, c; Elmer Angsman, b; Vince Banonis, c; Garrard Ramsey, g; Walter Szot, t; Mal Kutner, e; Stan Mauldin, t; Bill Dewell, e; Joe Coomer, t; Phil Handler, ass't coach; Ray C. Bennigsen, president.
3rd Row—(sitting) Bob Zimny, t; Loyd Arms, g; Marshall Goldberg, b; Walter Rankin, b; Jim Conzelman, head coach; Ray Apolskis, g; Charles Smith, b; Boris Dimancheff, b; Clarence Esser, e; Dick Plasman, ass't coach.

The Chicago Cardinals finished the 1947 season with a 9–3 record.

9

Highlight Reel

After 40 years in Chicago, the Cardinals moved to Saint Louis, Missouri, in 1960. The team started to play better. They won their division in 1974 and 1975. But, they lost in the first round of the play-offs both times.

In 1988, the Cardinals moved to Arizona. The team won seven games in its first season there. But, many players were injured. So the team did not make it to the play-offs.

The team's losing streak continued until 1998. That year, quarterback Jake Plummer led the team to nine wins. Then the team won its first play-off game in 51 years!

Star quarterback Jake Plummer played six seasons with the Cardinals.

Win or Go Home

NFL teams play 16 regular season games each year. The teams with the best records are part of the play-off games. Play-off winners move on to the conference championships. Then, conference winners face off in the Super Bowl!

In 2008, the Cardinals won the NFC **championship**. Then, they played in their first Super Bowl!

The Cardinals continued to have good seasons. They made it to the play-offs again in 2014 and 2015. Unfortunately, the Cardinals lost both times to the Carolina Panthers.

The Cardinals played the Pittsburgh Steelers in the 2009 Super Bowl. Sadly, the Cardinals lost 27–23.

Larry Fitzgerald Jr. is the youngest wide receiver in NFL history to have 1,000 **career** catches.

Halftime! Stat Break

Team Records

RUSHING YARDS
Career: Ottis Anderson, 7,999 yards (1979–1986)
Single Season: Ottis Anderson, 1,605 yards (1979)
PASSING YARDS
Career: Jim Hart, 34,639 yards (1966–1983)
Single Season: Carson Palmer, 4,671 yards (2015)
RECEPTIONS
Career: Larry Fitzgerald Jr., 1,018 receptions (2004–2015)
Single Season: Larry Fitzgerald, 109 receptions (2015)
ALL-TIME LEADING SCORER
Jim Bakken, 1,380 points (1963–1978)

Famous Coaches

Jimmy Conzelman
(1940–1942, 1946–1948)
Ken Whisenhunt (2007–2012)

Championships

EARLY CHAMPIONSHIP WINS:
1925, 1947

SUPER BOWL APPEARANCES:
2009

SUPER BOWL WINS:
None

14

STADIUM: University of Phoenix Stadium
LOCATION: Glendale, Arizona
MASCOT: Big Red

Pro Football Hall of Famers & Their Years with the Cardinals

Charles W. Bidwill Sr., Owner (1933–1947)
Jimmy Conzelman, Coach (1940–1942, 1946–1948)
Dan Dierdorf, Guard/Tackle (1971–1983)
John "Paddy" Driscoll, Quarterback (1920–1925)
Dick "Night Train" Lane, Cornerback (1954–1959)
Ollie Matson, Halfback (1952, 1954–1958)
Ernie Nevers, Fullback (1929–1931)
Jackie Smith, Tight End (1963–1977)
Charley Trippi, Halfback/Quarterback (1947–1955)
Roger Wehrli, Cornerback (1969–1982)
Aeneas Williams, Cornerback/Safety (1991-2000)
Larry Wilson, Free Safety (1960–1972)

Coaches' Corner

Ken Whisenhunt became head coach for the Cardinals in 2007. He coached the team for six seasons. Whisenhunt led the Cardinals to the 2009 Super Bowl. He is the most successful head coach in the team's history!

Before coaching, Whisenhunt played in the NFL for the Atlanta Falcons (*shown*), the New York Jets, and the Washington Redskins.

Bruce Arians became head coach of the Cardinals in 2013. He was named NFL Coach of the Year in 2014.

Star Players

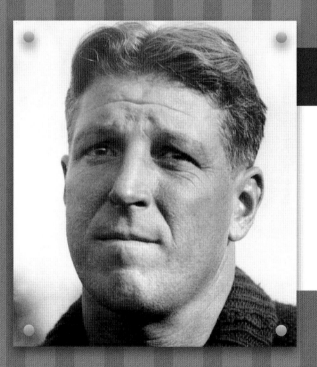

Ernie Nevers   FULLBACK (1929–1931)

Ernie Nevers was one of the first well-known football players. Nevers was known as a player who could do it all. He could run, pass, kick, and play defense with ease. Nevers became a member of the Pro Football Hall of Fame in 1963.

Roger Wehrli CORNERBACK (1969-1982)

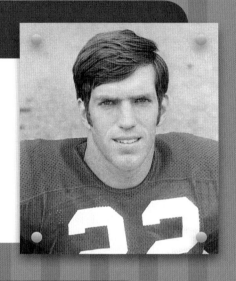

Roger Wehrli was the team's first-round pick in the 1969 **draft**. Over 14 seasons, he played 193 games and made 40 **interceptions**. Wehrli was selected to play in the Pro Bowl, which is the NFL's all-star game, seven times. He became a member of the Pro Football Hall of Fame in 2007.

Dan Dierdorf GUARD AND TACKLE (1971–1983)

The Cardinals drafted Dan Dierdorf in 1971. He was a smart, fast, and hard-working player. As a leader of the team's defense, he helped the Cardinals set records. Dierdorf played for the Cardinals his entire NFL **career**.

Aeneas Williams CORNERBACK AND SAFETY (1991–2000)

Aeneas Williams joined the Cardinals in 1991. He quickly became a star player. In his first game in the NFL, Williams made an **interception** and knocked away four passes. He ended the season by being named the NFC Defensive **Rookie** of the Year. Williams played for the Cardinals for ten seasons.

Pat Tillman SAFETY (1998–2001)

The Cardinals picked Pat Tillman in the 1998 **draft**. After the 2001 season, he decided to leave the NFL to join the United States Army. Sadly, Tillman was killed in action in 2004. To honor him, the team no longer uses number 40.

Larry Fitzgerald Jr. WIDE RECEIVER (2004–)

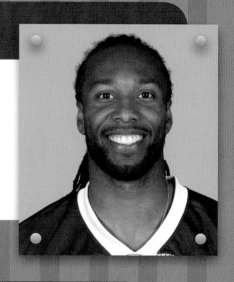

The Cardinals chose Larry Fitzgerald as the team's third-overall pick in the 2004 **draft**. He is a nine-time Pro Bowl pick. And, he was named the Pro Bowl Most Valuable Player (MVP) in 2008. Fitzgerald holds the team record for the most receptions in a single season.

Kurt Warner QUARTERBACK (2005–2009)

Kurt Warner joined the Cardinals in 2005. He led the team to the 2009 Super Bowl. Warner finished his **career** with the Cardinals passing for 15,843 yards and 100 touchdowns. Many consider him to be the best undrafted player of all time.

21

University of Phoenix Stadium

The Cardinals play home games at University of Phoenix Stadium. It is in Glendale, Arizona. University of Phoenix Stadium opened in 2006. It can hold 72,200 people.

The University of Phoenix Stadium was the first fully retractable grass field in North America.

Go Cards!

Thousands of fans flock to University of Phoenix Stadium to see the Cardinals play home games. In 1998, the team got a **mascot**. Big Red is a cardinal who wears jersey number 1. He helps fans cheer on the team!

Sound the Siren

In 2013, the Cardinals introduced the Big Red Siren. The Siren blows at the beginning of the game to introduce the Cardinals as they run onto the field.

Fans are called Red Sea Nation or the Bird Gang. Their slogan is "Protect the nest!"

The Cardinals have a long, rich history. They played in the 2009 Super Bowl. But, they are still waiting for their first Super Bowl win.

Even during losing seasons, true fans have stuck by them. Many believe the Arizona Cardinals will remain one of the greatest teams in the NFL.

The Cardinals have played in nine play-offs! Fans expect them to continue to succeed.

Through the Years

1898

The team starts when a group of men gather to play football.

1901

Owner Chris O'Brien buys used jerseys from the University of Chicago. He declares the faded jerseys are *cardinal red*. From then on the team is known as the Cardinals.

1920

The team is one of the first members of the NFL.

1925

The Cardinals win their first NFL **championship**.

1944

During **World War II**, the Cardinals combine with the Pittsburgh Steelers to play as one team. They call themselves the Card-Pitts.

1947

The Cardinals win their second NFL championship.

1974

The team wins ten games but loses to the Minnesota Vikings in the play-offs.

1988

The Cardinals move to Phoenix.

2009

The team plays in the Super Bowl for the first time.

1960

The Cardinals move to Saint Louis.

2015

The Cardinals lose to the Carolina Panthers in the NFC **championship**.

Postgame Recap

1. What is the name of the stadium where the Cardinals currently play home games?
   A. Sun Devil Stadium   **B.** U.S. Bank Stadium
   C. University of Phoenix Stadium

2. Name 3 of the 12 Cardinals players in the Pro Football Hall of Fame.

3. What year did the Cardinals move to Arizona?
   A. 1978   **B.** 1988   **C.** 1998

4. Where is the team's stadium located?
   A. Glendale, Arizona   **B.** Tempe, Arizona   **C.** Phoenix, Arizona

1. C. 2. See page 15 3. B. 4. A.

Glossary

career a period of time spent in a certain job.

championship a game, a match, or a race held to find a first-place winner.

draft a system for professional sports teams to choose new players. When a team drafts a player, they choose that player for their team.

interception (ihn-tuhr-SEHP-shuhn) when a player catches a pass that was meant for the other team's player.

mascot something to bring good luck and help cheer on a team.

rookie a first-year player in a professional sport.

World War II a war fought in Europe, Asia, and Africa from 1939 to 1945.

Websites

To learn more about the NFL's Greatest Teams, visit **booklinks.abdopublishing.com**. These links are routinely monitored and updated to provide the most current information available.

Index

7-17